GOD in the Shadows

The Revelation of His Kingdom

GARY FREY

Contents

Foreword

It was several years ago that Gary and I first met. Our family had been looking for a new church in our area and Gary was ministering and attending where we ended up. The fact that he was one of the first to welcome us and embrace us speaks to the love he carries in action. Through subsequent meetings over coffee and other times of fellowship, I discovered something about Gary. He has an incredible passion for God. Over the last several years I have met and known some incredible servants of the Lord but have met only a handful of people who are relentless in their pursuit of the Lord. Gary is one such person. Gary has a passion for the Lord Himself, not gifts, signs, opportunities, or anointings, but the Lord Jesus Himself. It is an honor to spend time with someone who loves the Lord in such a way and it has provoked me to keep the main thing the main thing. Over the last couple of years I have had the opportunity to bounce things off of Gary as I prepared and wrote some of my books. The book "School of the Supernatural" saw a vast rewrite due to Gary's input and I thank him for helping me to bring balance to a sometimes difficult subject. In this book, "God in the Shadows", Gary takes you on a journey to a place of intimacy with God. Stripping away the façade of religion and appearance, we go to a place where the Holy Spirit can lay bare our souls to look at the reality of our relationship and provoke us to the life in Christ we were meant to live. I pray you encounter God in the shadows.

-Michael Van Vlymen

Introduction

God in the Shadows, hidden from view, hidden from the casual observer, findable only by those whose hearts burn for Him. He is tucked away in the clutter of our circumstances, He whispers to us out of the overcasting details of everyday life, as well as from the midst of those overwhelming crises that arise from time to time. In each, and out of each is the calling fragrance that there is more; there is more here than what my senses can see. He draws me/us to come closer, to come where He resides. And as I approach nearer and nearer His shadow covers me, the brilliance of His person overwhelms me and I 'see' Him for who He is. I am humbled by how little I know Him. My Lord and my God, I hardly know You!

God is lurking in the midst of life, speaking to us in every possible situation and circumstance, and He desires that we KNOW Him above all things. We seem to think that He is primarily concerned in what we DO, when He is most concerned in our KNOWING Him. This short book has only one purpose and that is to provoke us to draw nearer to God, with the eternal promise that He will, in response, draw nearer to us. I pray you get that. Above all else, I pray you get that.

- G.F.

Chapter One

These People do not Know Me

I heard that all too familiar voice speak those words to me. "Which people, Lord?" was my initial thought. "Who are you speaking about?" And I suddenly 'knew' that He was speaking of this generation. There was neither anger nor disappointment in His voice, just a statement of fact.

In our western church we have become increasingly fragmented into movements and missions, pieces and parts, divisions and denominations, but rarely do we see the whole picture and vision that flows out of the heart of the Father. God wants **us** to know Him! As He showed and revealed Himself to His chosen people who were led by Moses, so He desires to reveal Himself to **us** through the Lord Jesus Christ... that **we** would **know** Him.

*Now this is eternal life: that they **know** you, the only true God, and Jesus Christ, whom you have sent. John 17:3 NIV*

However, we have developed a theology that people who have made a 'decision for Christ' now **do** in fact know Him. And yet, in spite of all our 'decisions' for God, the modern western church reflects more of the world around us than the world being impacted, influenced or changed by the church. In addition, the divisions, factions and disunity of the Church totally distort the image of the Lord Jesus Christ that the world sees. It is like looking at the image reflected back at us from a completely smashed mirror; we can see an image of some sort, but it is totally distorted.

Here is an interesting passage of scripture:

If someone says, "I love God," and yet hates his brother, he is a liar; for the one who does not love his brother whom he has seen, cannot love God whom he has not seen. 1 John 4:20

We could also take this even further and say that the one who is not willing to come into unity with his brother or sister in Christ, whom he or she can see, cannot possibly know God whom he or she has not seen. The Lord Jesus spoke and prophesied to His Father the importance of this true knowledge of God when He said,

*"My prayer is not for them alone. I pray also for those who will believe in me through their message, 21 **that all of them may be one**, Father, just as you are in me and I am in you. **May they also be in us** so that the world may believe that you have sent me. 22 I have given them the glory that you gave me, **that they may be one as we are one—** 23 I in them and you in me—so that they may be brought to complete unity. Then the world will know that you sent me and have loved them even as you have loved me. 24 "Father, **I want those you have given me to be with me where I am,** and to **see my glory**, the glory you have given me because you loved me before the creation of the world. 25 "Righteous Father, though the world does not know you, I know you, and they know that you have sent me. 26 **I have made you known to them, and will continue to make you known in order that the love you have for me may be in them and that I myself may be in them."** John 17:20-26 NIV*

Those words of the Father "These people do not know Me" continued to resonate within me. Again, I asked Him "Who are 'These people' that you are referring to, Lord?" And immediately I was reminded of these verses from Matthew's Gospel -

"Enter through the narrow gate; for the gate is wide and the way is broad that leads to destruction, and there are many

who enter through it. *14 For the gate is small and the way is narrow that leads to life, and there are few who find it. 15 "Beware of the false prophets, who come to you in sheep's clothing, but inwardly are ravenous wolves. 16 You will know them by their fruits. Grapes are not gathered from thorn bushes nor figs from thistles, are they? 17 So every good tree bears good fruit, but the bad tree bears bad fruit. 18 A good tree cannot produce bad fruit, nor can a bad tree produce good fruit. 19 Every tree that does not bear good fruit is cut down and thrown into the fire. 20 So then, you will know them by their fruits.*

21 "Not everyone who says to Me, 'Lord, Lord,' will enter the kingdom of heaven, but he who does the will of My Father who is in heaven will enter. 22 **Many will say to Me on that day, 'Lord, Lord, did we not prophesy in Your name, and in Your name cast out demons, and in Your name perform many miracles?'** *23 And then I will declare to them, 'I never knew you; depart from Me, you who practice lawlessness.' Matthew 7:13-23*

As I write these words, a sense of the awe and fear of the Lord has settled upon me. We claim such a familiarity with God, and yet we hardly know him. Bobby Connor said this a couple of years ago, and it seems to reflect where many of the Church resides today, *"We are way too familiar with a God we do not know!"*

Chapter Two

We Know About Him...

7 If you had known Me, you would have known My Father also; from now on you know Him, and have seen Him." Then Philip said to Him, "Lord, show us the Father, and it is enough for us." Jesus replied to him, "Have I been so long with you, and yet you have not come to know Me, Philip? He who has seen Me has seen the Father; how can you say, 'Show us the Father'? John 14:7-9

How is it possible for us to spend so much time with God in prayer, bible study, listening to messages, etc. and not really know Him. Is it possible that we hold back our lives from Him? That we withhold the deepest recesses of our hearts from His searching gaze?

Again, in Jesus' priestly prayer in John 17, He prayed the holy prayer that lives on today and will live on for eternity.

Now this is eternal life: that they **know** you, the only true God, and Jesus Christ, whom you have sent. John 17:3 NIV

The word 'know' used here in John 17 is from the Greek Word 'ginosko,' which means a progressive knowledge; also, to be taking in knowledge, to come to know, recognize, understand, or to understand completely. And it denotes a relationship between the object known and subject knowing.

Unless we 'know' God we will not live with Him in eternity. It is just that simple. In spite of all our great learning, great teachings, books, radio and TV programs, authors and teachers, prophets and apostolic peoples, we know more **about** Him than we know Him.

Here is what the great Twentieth Century prophet, A.W. Tozer had to say on this subject of knowing God,

"Now this is eternal life: that they **know** you, the only true God, and Jesus Christ, whom you have sent. John 17:3. We have but to introduce one extra word into this verse to see how vast is the difference between knowing 'about' and 'knowing'. "This is eternal life, that they might know **about** you, the only true God, and Jesus Christ, whom You have sent." (The natural) man, by reason, cannot know God, he can only know about Him." From 'The Divine Conquest'

I can listen to my best friend tell me all about his wife, and I can look at her picture, even read her biography, and yet I will not 'know' her. I will know about her. And even if I meet my best friends wife, and spend quality time with her, I will not know her as my friend does. He knows her deeply and intimately in a way and manner that I will never experience. So it is with God. We can read the scriptures from Genesis to Revelation, and learn much about Him. But, until we cross that threshold of relationship with Him, and draw near to Him, we will not know Him; we will only know **about** Him.

But, the promises of God very clearly point to Him, that IF we seek Him, search for Him, draw close to Him, long for Him, and profess our desire for Him, HE WILL come closer and closer to us. I have stated this many times, and I'll continue to declare it in this book: we can be as close to God as we desire. We determine the depth of our intimate relationship with Him. No one else, just us.

"This is **ETERNAL LIFE**, that they **KNOW** You, the One true God, and Jesus Christ the One whom You sent." John 17:3 NIV

Jesus said to him, "I am the way, and the truth, and the **LIFE**; no one comes to the Father but through Me. 7 If you had **KNOWN** Me, you would have **KNOWN** My Father also;

from now on you **KNOW** Him, and have seen Him." Philip *said to Him, "Lord, show us the Father, and it is enough for us." Jesus said to him, **"Have I been so long with you, and yet you have not come to KNOW Me, Philip?** He who has seen Me has seen the Father" John 14:6-9 (Emphasis mine)

Can you hear the disappointment and exasperation in the words of Jesus? Philip, one of the twelve, and one who had journeyed with the Lord for over three years, one who ate with Him, slept with Him, and who listened and watched Him every moment of every day, did not know the real Jesus. Many today would say, "Oh, if I could only have spent three years with the Lord, I know I would not have made that same mistake."

But, the reality of our human existence is that we tend to 'judge' all things by our natural senses and perceptions. It takes years for the work of the Holy Spirit to remove our hidden prejudices and biases. The disciples of Jesus only 'knew' Him with their natural understanding. Yes, Peter had the revelation that He was the Christ, but even he didn't understand that the Christ must suffer death on a cross. Their collective eyes were not fully opened to the true nature of the Lord Jesus until they received the Holy Spirit, (John 20:22), and were baptized by the Holy Spirit. (Acts 2:1-4) And even after that it was years before the revelation of Christ the risen Lord, the image of the Father, and Christ in us came to be released through Paul, Peter and John.

"...in those who **know Him** there is a quiet restful strength which speaks of a great depth of life... Let me point out that in Christ 'are all the treasures of wisdom and knowledge hidden,' and the Lord's will for us is to come to an everlasting realization and personal appreciation of Him in Whom all the **fullness** dwells... The absence of this real **knowledge of the Lord** has proven to be the most tragic factor in the Church's history." **T. Austin-Sparks**

"But the people who **KNOW** their God shall be strong, and carry out great exploits." Daniel 11:32 NKJV

IN OUR IMAGE AND LIKENESS

Then God said, "Let Us make man in **Our image**, according to **Our likeness**." Genesis 1:26 NKJV

For those whom He foreknew, He also predestined to **become conformed to the image of His Son**, so that He would be the firstborn among many brethren. Romans 8:29

The Son is the dazzling radiance of God's splendor, the **exact expression** of God's true nature—**His mirror image!** Hebrews 1:3 The Passion Translation (TPT)

But we all, with unveiled face, beholding as in a mirror the glory of the Lord, **are being transformed into the same image** from glory to glory, just as from the Lord, the Spirit. 2 Corinthians 3:18

THE FULLNESS OF GOD

"In Him dwells all the **FULLNESS** of the Deity, and you (plural) have been given **FULLNESS** in Christ..." Colossians 2:9, 10 NIV 1984

"...that you may come to know, practically, through experience for yourself the love of Christ, which far surpasses mere knowledge without experience, that you may be filled up throughout all your being unto all the **FULLNESS** of God, so that you may have the richest measure and experience of God's presence in your lives, that you would be **completely filled and flooded with God Himself.** Ephesians 3:19 AMP

As We Become Conformed Into His Image and Likeness We Become His Representative Body

EVERYTHING that was prophesied and proclaimed about the Son of Man, and that was manifested in and through His life, both before the cross and after His resurrection, EVERYTHING about His life will be manifested in and through the many-membered body of Christ; EVERYTHING!

"Truly, truly, I say to you, **he who believes in Me, the works that I do, he will do also; and greater works than these he will do; because I go to the Father**. Whatever you ask in My name, that will I do, so that the Father may be glorified in the Son. If you ask Me anything in My name, I will do it. John 14:12-14

"You can never give another person that which you have found, but you can make him homesick for what you have." **Oswald Chambers**

Chapter Three

Only the Holy Spirit Can Reveal the True Knowledge of God to Us

"I keep asking that the God of our Lord Jesus Christ, the glorious Father, may give you the Spirit of **wisdom and revelation**, so that you may **know him better.** I pray that the eyes of your heart may be enlightened in order that you may know the hope to which he has called you, the riches of his glorious inheritance in his holy people, and his incomparably great power for us who believe." Ephesians 1:17-19 - NIV

Jesus said that no one could come to Him, (be drawn to Him, or get to know Him), except the (Spirit of the) Father draw him, (see John 6:44). The Father and the Son want us to know them. And it is the Holy Spirit who reveals them to us. How? As we seek God we find Him. As we draw near to God, He draws near to us. As we seek to love, He gives us love. As we seek unity among the brethren, He releases to us the 'spirit of unity.' And as we seek FIRST the Realm of the Kingdom of God, ALL of the other things we desire - the basic needs of life, as well as the unique attributes of the Kingdom life (gifts of the Spirit, signs, wonders and miracles) are added to us as well. Wow!

When We Begin to 'See' and 'Know'

When we begin to 'see' and 'know' Jesus Christ as He is then we will begin to see the Realm of the Kingdom and to enter in.

Jesus answered him, "I assure you and most solemnly say to you, unless a person is **born again [reborn from above— spiritually transformed, renewed, sanctified]**, he

cannot [ever] **see and experience** the kingdom of God."
John 3:3 AMP

Jesus answered, "I assure you and most solemnly say to you, unless one is **born of water and the Spirit** he cannot [ever] **enter** the kingdom of God. John 3:5 AMP

The Lord Jesus is the Kingdom of God. Where He is there lies the kingdom. He is the righteousness of God, He is the peace of God, He is the joy of God, He is the wisdom of God and He is the power of God. In Him dwells all the fullness of God. (See Colossians 2:9) And unless we truly KNOW Him, we will not see, enter or experience the realm of the kingdom. We may even be able operate in the gifts of the Spirit, but we will not know Him...

"So above all, constantly chase after the **Realm of God's Kingdom** and the righteousness that proceeds from Him. Then all these less important things will be given to you abundantly. Matthew 6:33 - The Passion Translation (TPT)

The Lord Jesus said some amazing things to those who were closest to Him. These were the men who had spent three years with Him in the full spectrum of life. He knew them well. And still they barely knew Him, as evidenced by the exchange between He and Phillip. (John 14:9) They thought they knew Him, but they were trapped in the limited knowledge of rational understanding. He wanted them, (and us), to know Him deeply and intimately. And I dare say more so than what most of us today have wanted to know Him.

Listen to His passionate words,

"He who has My commandments (words, sayings) and keeps them, it is he who loves Me. And he who loves Me will be loved by My Father, and I will love him and **manifest (show, reveal, make known)**, Myself to him." John 14:21 AMPC

And then,

"If a person [really] loves Me, he will keep My word [obey My teaching]; and My Father will love him, **and We will come to him and make Our home (abode, special dwelling place) with him.** John 14:23 AMPC

These words of Jesus have taken life in my heart for years now. Oh, how I want to know Him better. I can better understand Paul's words in Philippians 3,

"But more than that, I count everything as loss compared to the priceless privilege and supreme advantage of knowing Christ Jesus my Lord [and of growing more deeply and thoroughly acquainted with Him—a joy unequaled]. For His sake I have lost everything, and I consider it all garbage, so that I may gain Christ, And this, so that I may know Him [experientially, becoming more thoroughly acquainted with Him, understanding the remarkable wonders of His Person more completely] and [in that same way experience] the power of His resurrection [which overflows and is active in believers], and [that I may share] the fellowship of His sufferings, by being continually conformed [inwardly into His likeness even] to His death [dying as He did]; so that I may attain to the resurrection [that will raise me] from the dead. Not that I have already obtained it [this goal of being Christlike] or have already been made perfect, but I actively press on so that I may take hold of that [perfection] for which Christ Jesus took hold of me and made me His own." Philippians 3:8,10-12 AMP

Paul wrote these words towards the end of his life. He wasn't stating that he wished he could go on more mission trips, reach more people, make more disciples or win more lost people. He was stating that he longed to 'know Him better... to take hold of Christ as He took hold of me...."

Chapter Four

An 'Angel' Named Charlie

I first saw him walking out of a local convenience store. He was an older black man pulling an airline travel bag and had another bag over his shoulder. I knew immediately that he was homeless, homeless in a community that does not have a homeless population.

Before I could stop myself I asked him if I could give him a ride somewhere. He stared at me for a few seconds, and then nodded his head and said, "I guess that would be alright."

He was only traveling a half mile of so down the road. As we drove he confirmed that he was indeed 'homeless.' He also let me know that he was a veteran. I asked him if he was hungry, and he said not too bad, but he could use some snacks.

After I bought him a few things, I found out he wasn't working with the VA, and didn't have anybody trying to help him. Again, against all better judgment I told him I would try to help him. This was the beginning of a life changing, yet tumultuous and insanely hard journey. I'd like to share that with you, if you'll hang around long enough to let me finish.

I'm a white middle class middle-aged believer in Jesus Christ. I was radically saved in a wonderful encounter with the Holy Spirit in 1982. There was a strong element of total surrender to the Lord when I was born again, and yet, there was still so much of Gary that remained in me, and that would continue to sabotage my life over the next thirty years. Much of it I am filled with regret. However, about eight years ago this aging middle class white man determined that he wanted to know God, the Lord, the Lord Jesus, and the Holy Spirit as well as they would let me come to them. I heard the Lord say to me,

"You can come as close to me as you want, if you are willing to pay that price."

Oh yes, I want to come close, Lord! I am ready. What do you want from me? I heard in the still small voice in my deepest place, "All of you." With little thought as to what I was saying, I replied, "It's all yours."

And so began a journey that has continued into years now. The Holy Spirit ever so gently began to confront me with me, with my carnal life, my pervasive self, that wants to control and dominate every aspect of who I am. There were 'dark nights' and 'dark days,' wilderness and surrender, and then we would do it all over again. I gradually was pulled away from almost every form of ministry that I had been engaged in just so the Lord could finish what He had started, and what I had ventured to say that I wanted.

After years and years of breaking, and months of isolation I sensed things actually shifting. I was no longer dominated by my own life's thoughts, questioning what were my gifts and callings; instead I found myself, like Paul in Philippians 3, crying out, "I want to know Him, and the power of His resurrection and the fellowship of His suffering." I was finally there. I believed I was no longer consumed with me, but I was ready to just be identified with Christ in His death, burial and resurrection. Or so I thought...

Then I met "Charlie," a homeless, toothless, broke and down and out man that the Holy Spirit has used to take me into the deepest places of my heart, places I couldn't reach on my own.

After that first day when I met "Charlie", (not his real name, but he's a real person), I did some research on what he might be eligible for through the Veteran's Administration, (also called the VA.) We made several trips to the local VA Hospital in our area, got him medical and mental exams, and explored some housing options. In the meantime, "Charlie" mentioned that he didn't have any place to take a shower or wash his clothes. I felt the Holy Spirit nudge me, "Invite him to use your place."

So, Charlie came over, washed his clothes and took a shower. Two days later he was back, and he asked me if he could shower again, spend the night and go to church with me. How could I say no to that? The next day, on the way back from church, he asked me what I was going to do the rest of the day. I just wanted to be alone, (and I for sure did not want his company,) so I told him I had some things to do. I could tell he wanted to stay at my place some more. But, I dropped him off at the local McDonalds, and I drove home.

As I'm pulling away from McDonalds, the Holy Spirit said, *"You weren't honest with him. Tomorrow I want you to invite him to stay with you for as long as he needs to."*

Gulp! "Yes, Lord!"

Charlie quickly proved himself to be one of the grossest, most obnoxious men I have ever been around. Because he had no teeth he made a lot of noise when he ate. There was a maximum of slurping, lip smacking, and other hard to describe noises as he ate, drank and consumed large quantities of food.

I also quickly discovered that Charlie could be very critical of me and my house. In a matter of no time he pointed out that my floor needed to be swept, that my refrigerator was dirty and that my bathroom needed to be cleaned. As it turned out, Charlie was very OCD about cleanliness. He may have been homeless, but he was neat and clean. So, his critical comments about my place didn't go over well. Oh, but, there was more to come.

I found that Charlie could only talk or ask for something by barking, or asking in a very demanding tone of voice. He also didn't know certain words, such as 'thanks, or thank you,' or

21

please, or anything that acknowledged what I was doing for him. Everything was an expectation.

One evening a few weeks after he began to stay with me, I fixed dinner for the two of us. I endured being at the table with him, although I found my stomach a little queasy with all of his eating noises. After we ate, he volunteered to wash the dishes, and I decided to go for a walk. When I came back he was standing outside smoking a little cigar. As I walked past him, I reached out to pat him on the shoulder and started to say thanks for cleaning the kitchen. Before I could speak he pulled away from me and squared off as if to hit me.

"What are you doing?" I exclaimed, in my most magnificently offended, self righteous voice! He replied, "I don't let no one touch me!"

"Are you kidding me?" I replied, "After all I've done for you, and you don't trust me by now?!" (Oh, I was in rare form, for sure!) "If you don't' trust me then just get your stuff and get out!" Oh, yes, I was that self righteous!

I walked back into my house fuming. Immediately, I knew the Lord was ready to respond. Before He had a a chance I said, "I am not apologizing. I am not!" He said nothing.

As soon as I woke up the next morning, the Holy Spirit said, *"You know you're going to apologize to him, don't you?"* "Yes, Sir," I replied.

And that was the beginning of the Holy Spirit teaching me that Charlie wasn't in my life for me to help him, but the Holy Spirit had sent him to help me.

Oh, my!

Over the next few months time and time again, Charlie pushed me to the max, every 'button' in me that could be pushed, he pushed. If I was a control panel, all of my lights would be lit up! And, of course, I responded as any 'normal' person would. I would get offended, declare that he had to go, pray that he would get settled so that my 'thorn in the flesh' would be removed, etc.

We finally got a call one day, and a space in a VA group home opened up for him. Our 'relationship' had become so strained that he actually left me and slept on the streets for a few days. He couldn't wait to get away from me. I have to admit that I missed him a little bit, but it was so nice to have my house back to myself.

When we got to the group home, as he was filling out the necessary paperwork to stay there, he was asked if there was anyone that he wanted to put on the 'authorized to visit' list. "Nah," he said, "I can't think of nobody." His counselor said, "Well, what about Gary?" (Mind you, I was in the room with them.) "Nah, I got no use for him no more. I'm done with him."

W.O.W.!

Pain, hurt, anguish, sadness, deep feelings of being unappreciated, oh, I could go on. How could this man that I had invested so much into with time and money say such a thing?

The Holy Spirit finally had to remind me that I did all those things as unto Him, not Charlie. That helped some.

My place seemed very quiet after he was gone. I continued to pray for him, knowing that there was so much that the Lord wanted to do for Charlie.

A week or so later, to my complete surprise, my front door opened and in walked Charlie. He was grinning with his toothless grin, and said, "Hey, can I come back?" "What happened to your group home?" I asked. "Aw, man, them dudes were filthy! I couldn't stand that place."

"And what about what you said to me where you checked in there, that you had no use for me anymore?"

"Man, I never said that..."

And that's where I discovered that Charlie had multiple personalities. Yes, he was clinically schizophrenic, anti-social, paranoid, and OCD. Other than that he was fine.

Over the next few weeks the Lord began to speak to me about interceding for Charlie. I was invited to 'take him on' as an object of intercession.

I had read some about intercession, and as much as I knew from reading about it, including the amazing story of Rees Howells, and his son Samuel, I still knew almost nothing. I knew that you must identify with the person or thing you are interceding for, and that the Holy Spirit will expose every single weakness you have. There can be nothing in you that the enemy can lay hold of you to accuse you with.

"Will you do this", He asked. I agreed, still not fully understanding what I was getting into.

Over the next few weeks Charlie, once again, manifested every quality that he had which could push my buttons. His dark side became darker, and "Good Charlie" was rarely seen. Once again he wanted to fight me, this time because I looked at him.

He finally said he had had enough of me and wanted to leave again. So he left. I knew he'd be back.

And seven days later he returned, again, promising to be better. But, in a matter of days he was reverting back to his old ways.

I wanted to throw him out! "I want him out of my life, Lord! I can't stand him!" *"See,"* the Holy Spirit said, *"There's still a lot of you in you."* I groaned as I realized this was still going to take a while.

"Oh, Lord, help me die!"

The Lord said, *"I want you to see and treat Charlie as if he's royalty. I died for him just as I did for you. I love him just as I love you."*

Wow, did that sink deep!

I began to keep my mouth shut around Charlie. I fixed great meals for him, and made sure he had everything he needed. I had to fight myself almost daily to not respond to him. I just prayed, fasted, confessed the word of God, declared over him that he belonged to the Lord Jesus Christ.

I felt led of the Lord to start having regular prayer meetings in my home. A few friends and I gathered every couple weeks in my house to pray for revival for our area. But, I thought to myself, 'what should I do about Charlie?'

I decided to invite him to share in our pitch-in dinner before the meeting, and then he could do what he wanted. The first meeting he didn't eat with us, or even hang around. But, the next meeting he not only ate with us, but listened in to the entire prayer meeting. And the following meeting he actually was engaging with the people, and again sat in during the prayer meeting.

Not once did we try to draw him in, pray for him, or involve him. It just wasn't the time.

During all this time Charlie and I tolerated each other. He really didn't want to talk very much, and I was perfectly okay with that. Even though I was consciously interceding for him, all I could think about was the day when he would be leaving. "How long, Lord?" And I 'heard,' *"As long as it takes for you to get it!"* Another groan...

At the next prayer meeting it was Charlie's sixtieth birthday. I surprised him with a cake, and gave him a birthday card that everybody present had signed. Then we sang happy birthday to him. I saw Charlie smile like never before. And this time Charlie sat right in our prayer circle, and listened intently to every word said or prayed. His demeanor seemed noticeably softer, and he even allowed a few people to hug him goodby.

A couple of days later I was praying for him, and wondering when the shoe was going to drop, when "Bad Charlie" would re-emerge. All of a sudden, the Holy Spirit reminded me of this passage out of Romans: "(as it is written, "I have made you a father of many nations") in the presence of Him whom he believed—**God, who gives life to the dead and calls those things which do not exist as though they did**" Romans 4:17 - NKJV

"I want you to begin calling out and prophesying over Charlie that he is a son of God, and that he is free." I became very convicted that I had been hindering the Lord from working in Charlie's life by my constant murmuring and complaining about him to myself.

So, I began prophesying and declaring over Charlie that he was saved in the name of the Lord Jesus Christ, that he was a son of God, and that he was free from all the strongholds that lived in him. And I spoke peace over him.

The results were immediate and dramatic. That very day he spoke to me from a place of respect, thanking me for a little thing I did for him.

A few weeks later, Charlie left. We had come to the end of our time together. The VA was giving him a place of his own, and so I said my goodbyes. He finally thanked me for all I had done for him, I prayed over him and he left.

I didn't have any contact with Charlie for sixteen months, then out of the blue he called me. We spoke for 15 or 20 minutes, and it was the most lucid conversation we had ever had. He's in a place of his own, has some income, is attending a church, and exhibited a small measure of peace he hadn't had before. I will continue to present Charlie before the Lord. I know there's more for him.

But God's work in Charlie was also what He did in me. He used another to shine the light of His presence down deep into the deepest, and darkest recesses of my one heart. Out of the shadows of my own heart I found the true heart and nature of the One I seek. I came to 'know' Him as my true life.

Chapter Five

The Promise of God

We love to quote and meditate all of God's promises, but perhaps His greatest promise is not what we can get from Him, but that we can actually know personally and corporately the God of the universe. This continues to blow me away more than any other thing.

Come close to God [with a contrite heart] and He will come close to you. Wash your hands, you sinners; and purify your [unfaithful] hearts, you double-minded [people]. Be miserable and grieve and weep [over your sin]. Let your [foolish] laughter be turned to mourning and your [reckless] joy to gloom. Humble yourselves [with an attitude of repentance and insignificance] in the presence of the Lord, and He will exalt you [He will lift you up, He will give you purpose]. James 4:8-10 AMP

God's promise to us, and this is written all through the scriptures, is that if we will seek Him, we will find Him.

*You will **seek** me and find me when you search for me with **all your heart. I will be found by you**" Jeremiah 29:13,14 NIV*

*And without faith it is impossible to please Him, for he who comes to God must believe that He is and that He is a rewarder of those who **seek** Him. Hebrews 11:6*

How does He reward us, you say? With the knowledge of Himself.

A few years ago I was in a season of really seeking more of God, really seeking to draw close to Him. My heart was bursting with the desire to truly 'know' Him better. The Holy Spirit prompted me one day to walk over to my bookcase and stand in front of it. Then He said, *"Everything you are seeking right now is in front of you."* I knew he was speaking about a book or books in my bookcase, but which one? Suddenly I was drawn to The Final Quest, by Rick Joyner. I had read the book a few times and recalled that in his vision that The Final Quest recounted, the Lord Jesus had several long conversations with the author. As I read these words that Jesus spoke to him in the book, it was as if the Lord was speaking them directly to me.

Here are a few:

"You think like Me when you are in perfect union with Me...

"You can be just as close to Me as anyone has ever been to Me, and even more. I have made the way for everyone to be as close to Me as they truly desire to be. If you really desire to be closer to Me that even Paul was, you can. Some will want this, and they will want it badly enough to lay aside anything that hinders their intimacy with Me, to give themselves fully to it, and they will have what they seek...

"I want to be much closer to you, and to everyone who calls upon Me, than I have yet been able to be with anyone who has ever lived. You determine how close we will be, not I. I will be found by those who seek Me..."

But the one who is united and joined to the Lord is one spirit with Him. 1 Corinthians 6:17 AMP

We are called to know Him, to be conformed into His image, to reflect His glory, to live as His ambassadors in this life, to carry about in our bodies the dying of Jesus so that the life of Jesus might be revealed in our mortal, (created, yet dying) bodies. We are one with Him in spirit, we are called to be one with one another as His body, we are one with His mind, and He wants us to know His heart and His soul. **He wants us to know Him!**

*"May He grant you out of the rich treasury of His glory to be strengthened and reinforced with mighty power in the inner man by the [Holy] Spirit [Himself indwelling your innermost being and personality].17 May Christ through your faith [actually] dwell (settle down, abide, make His permanent home) in your hearts! May you be rooted deep in love and founded securely on love,18 That you may have the power and be strong to apprehend and grasp with all the saints [God's devoted people, the experience of that love] what is the breadth and length and height and depth [of it]; 19 [That you may really come] to **know** [practically, through experience for yourselves] the love of Christ, which far surpasses mere knowledge [without experience]; that you may be filled [through all your being] unto all the fullness of God **[may have the richest measure of the divine Presence, and become a body wholly filled and flooded with God Himself]! Ephesians 3:16-19 AMPC***

This is the true knowledge of God. We, this generation, have a hunger for the 'more' of God that's seems greater than any generation before us. We want to do great exploits FOR Him, but we barely know Him. There is so much more to God than we can even comprehend. Those who seek Him and begin to know Him better all begin to realize that the more we know Him, how little we in fact do know Him.

Here is some more of what A. W. Tozer said:

"To have found God and still to pursue Him is the soul's paradox of love, scorned indeed by the too-easily satisfied religionists, but justified in happy experience by the children of the burning heart... (and if you) come near to the holy men and women of the past, you will soon feel the heat of their desire after God. They mourned for Him, they prayed and

wrestled and sought for Him day and night, in season and out, and when they had found Him the finding was all the more sweeter for the long seeking." The Pursuit of God, A.W. Tozer

"These people do not know Me, but I want them to. And they will, if they seek Me and pursue Me." The Father

And listen to what Brother Sadhu Sundar Selveraj says in his book, **Last Days Seven Horn Anointing,**

*"For it says, "but the people who **know** their God shall be strong, and carry out great exploits." Daniel 11:32 Before you can do great exploits for God, you must **intimately know** God. Not just know about God but have an intimate experiential relationship with God. The word, "know" in Hebrew is yada and means to know by observation, that is, to know God by being close to Him through an experiential and intimate relationship. The word, "strong" in Hebrew is chazaq and means to fasten upon, be courageous, to conquer. Putting it all together, the phrase, "but the people who know their God shall be strong, and carry out great exploits" means:* **When you have a real relationship with God that is built upon an intimate knowing of Him and His ways, you become one with His will.** *That becoming one with Him will make you strong and courageous against all the powers of the enemy that he will unleash in these last days. Before you can do any great exploits (for God), you must be a person who walks with God." (Emphasis mine)*

FINAL THOUGHTS

"My brethren, count it all joy when you fall into various trials, knowing that the testing of your faith produces patience. But let patience have its perfect work, that you may be **perfect and complete, lacking nothing. James 1:2-4 NKJV** (Emphasis mine)

Everything that happens and transpires to us, all of the profound circumstances that seem to constantly be knocking at our door, and all of the trials, test, events in our lives, have one purpose: to shape us, change us, and reveal to us our true nature and character. To one who is committed to God, who is purposefully pursuing Him as their Life, there are no accidents in their pursuit. Nothing is happening because of 'fate' or happenstance. God is in the middle of all things. His one purpose is that we enter into His kingdom as His sons and daughters, his inheritance, made in the likeness of His Son, Jesus, and that we are fully complete and we are lacking nothing in the Kingdom of God.

If we say that we love Him, then we must also know Him. We will not have the true unity and oneness in the body of Christ until we both individually and corporately know Him. He is calling us to **KNOW** Him! And He wants from us the full value of what He has paid for. A people who fully belong to Him, and Him alone. Will you/we answer that call? In order to truly live in the realm of His Kingdom we must know Him.

Where we are TODAY is where the Lord has placed us so that we can know Him better and experience His kingdom. The kingdom is a person, and that kingdom/person lives in you, assuming you pass the test. (2 Corinthians 13:5). Every circumstance, every person, every trial; test and tribulation are present in your life to bring you closer to God, that you might know Him better. If we give thanks to God in ALL circumstances, and in ALL situations, if we count it all joy for the testing of our faith, we may be overwhelmingly surprised at how much we come to 'know' God in the Father, in the Son, and in the Holy Spirit. For the God in the shadows so desires that you know Him above all things.

Selah

www.ingramcontent.com/pod-product-compliance
Lightning Source LLC
Chambersburg PA
CBHW071940020426
42331CB00010B/2950